GIVE THE *Bitch* HER CHOCOLATE

THE *Feisty Foodie* EDITION

GIVE THE *Bitch* HER CHOCOLATE

Ed Polish * Darren Wotz

TEN SPEED PRESS
Berkeley | Toronto

Thanks to Veronica Randall, Betsy Stromberg, Ben Truwe, Bryan Howell, and the late, lamented Ray Guadagnino. Boundless love to Ginny Polish. Vast gratitude to the indefatigable gang at Ephemera, Inc.

Check out Ephemera, Inc. at www.ephemera-inc.com

Ten Speed Press
PO Box 7123
Berkeley, California 94707
www.tenspeed.com

Distributed in Australia by Simon and Schuster Australia, in Canada by Ten Speed Press Canada, in New Zealand by Southern Publishers Group, in South Africa by Real Books, and in the United Kingdom and Europe by Publishers Group UK.

Cover and text design by Betsy Stromberg and Ed Polish

Library of Congress Cataloging-in-Publication Data

Polish, Ed.
  Give the bitch her chocolate : the feisty foodie edition / Ed Polish, Darren Wotz.
    p. cm.
  ISBN 1-58008-974-7 (978-1-58008-974-6 : alk. paper)
  1. Women—Humor. 2. Food—Humor. I. Wotz, Darren. II. Title.
  PN6231.W6P64 2009
  741.5'973—dc22

                           2008041472

Printed in China
First printing, 2009

1 2 3 4 5 6 7 8 9 10 — 13 12 11 10 09

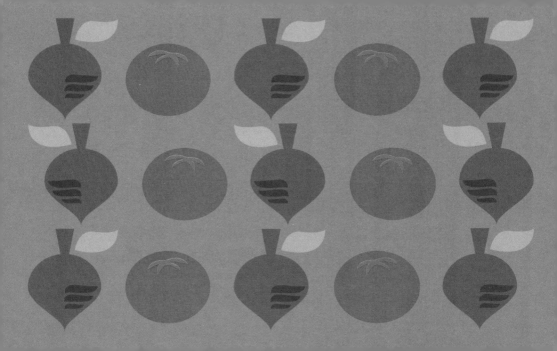

Try Organic Food

...or as your grandparents called it, "Food"

UNATTENDED CHILDREN WILL BE GIVEN ESPRESSO AND A FREE KITTEN

WORLD PEACE,
MULTIPLE
ORGASMS,
and
FANCY DARK
CHOCOLATE,
in that order

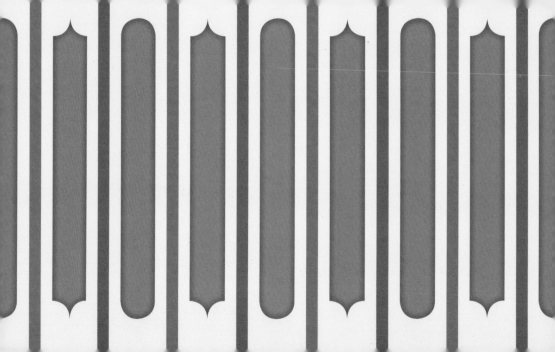

I AM ONLY
AS STRONG AS
THE MARTINIS
I DRINK
&
THE HAIRSPRAY
I USE

BECAUSE CHOCOLATE DOESN'T LEAVE A WET SPOT

DRINK COFFEE—

do stupid things faster with more energy.

The glass can
be half empty
...or half full...

as long as
there's Scotch
in it.

If we are
what we eat,
I'm fast,
cheap,
and easy.

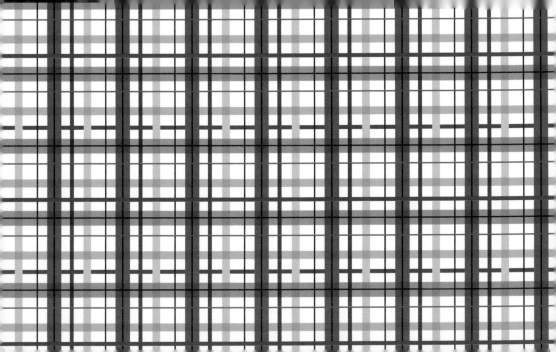

MEAT IS MURDER!

TASTY, TASTY MURDER.

FUDGE

A great palate cleanser after her date with Brad.

I Always Take Life with a Grain of Salt, plus a Slice of Lime and a Shot of Tequila

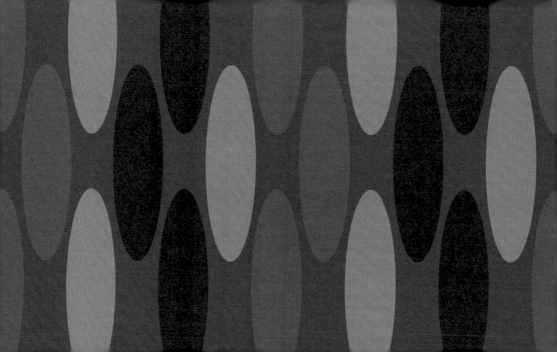

You, me . . .
and a gallon of
chocolate syrup.

Wait.

Forget about you!

I could
learn to cook—
but why risk
chipping
a nail?

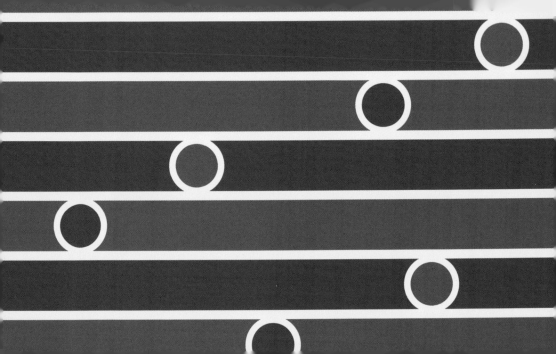

EATING
MY WEIGHT
IN CHOCOLATE
ICE CREAM
HELPS ME
COPE

If we're not supposed to eat animals,
how come they're made out of meat?

The
Ozone Layer
or Cheese in
a Spray Can?

Don't
Make Me
Choose!

PLEASE
IGNORE
THE URINE
SMELL

When it was that time of the month, Nancy could bite your head off and eat a Twinkie at the same time.

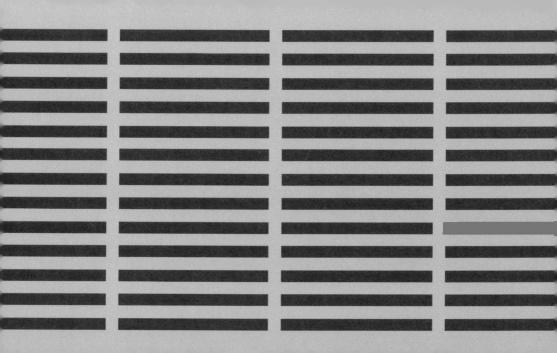

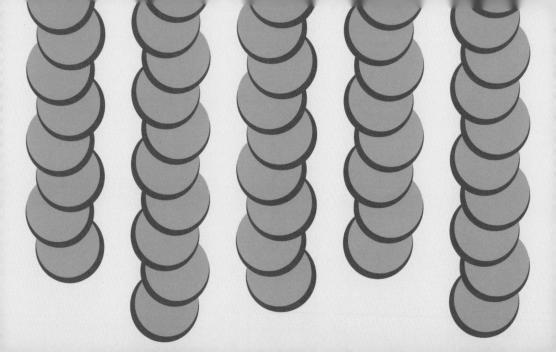

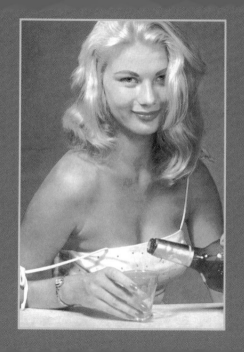

TEQUILA!
Because Beer Isn't Fast Enough!

MADGE'S POT BROWNIES WERE A HIT AT THE CHURCH SOCIAL

Iris loved springtime, when she could open the windows and air out the smell of Frank's beer farts.

EAT A SQUARE MEAL A DAY—

A BOX OF CHOCOLATES

IN A PERFECT WORLD ALL MEN WOULD BE PASTRY CHEFS

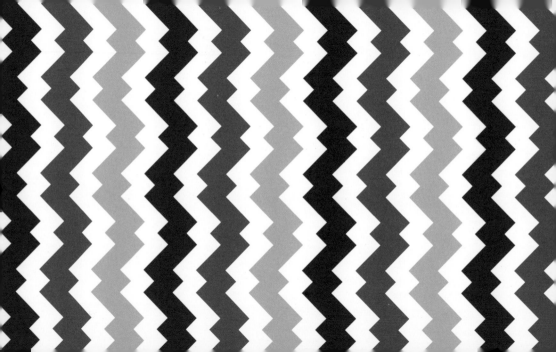

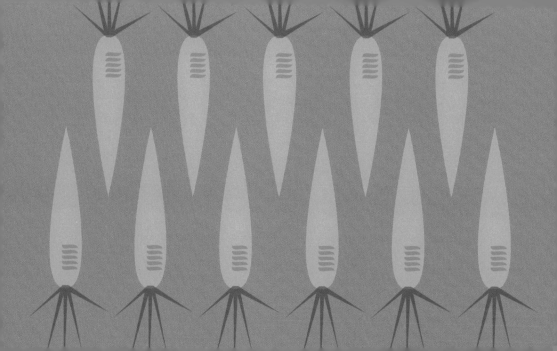

Easy there,
Mr. Testosterone—

You can
be replaced
by a zucchini.

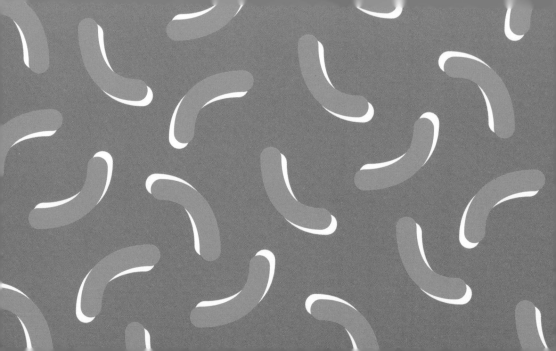

STEP AWAY
FROM THE
FRIDGE,
LARDASS.

Explain to me again why I shouldn't eat my young.

No Pulse Yet...

More Coffee, Please.

BEER!

NOT JUST
FOR
BREAKFAST
ANYMORE

IF IT FITS IN A TOASTER, I CAN COOK IT

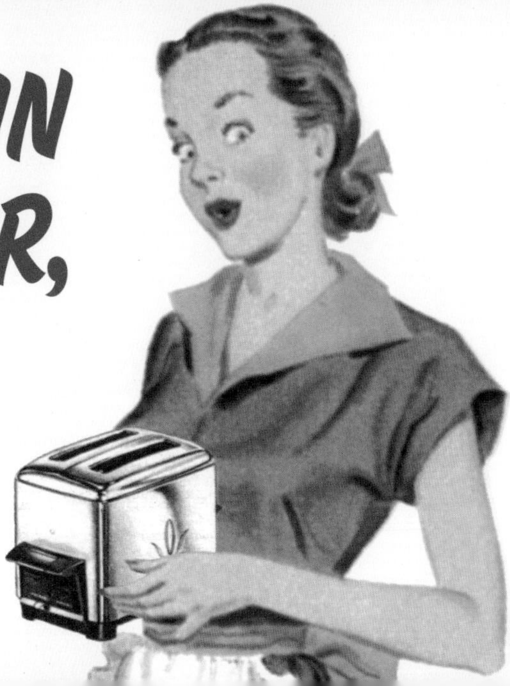

It's not nagging when I have the butcher knife, dear.

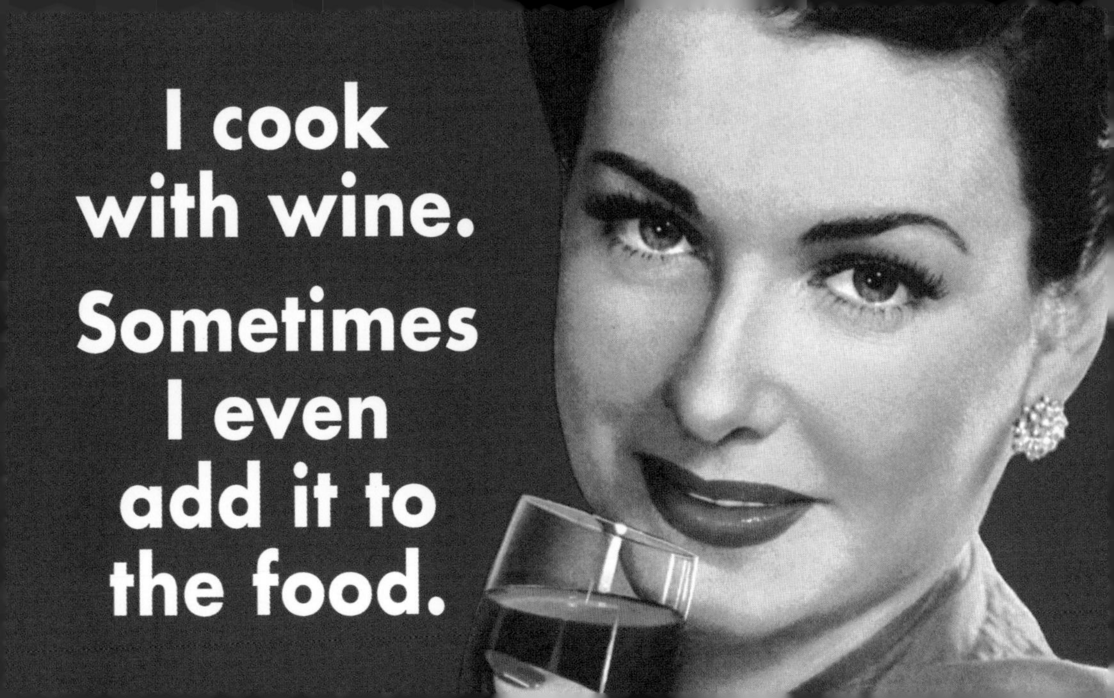
I cook
with wine.
Sometimes
I even
add it to
the food.

A COUPLE MORE ESPRESSOS AND I CAN FLY!

BEER WILL CHANGE THE WORLD

I don't know how, but it will

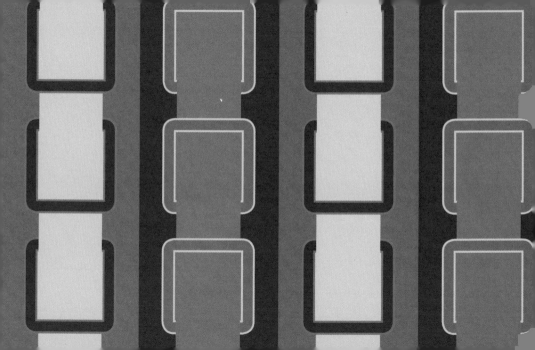

TOFU!

Looks like
wallpaper
paste
but tastes
much worse!

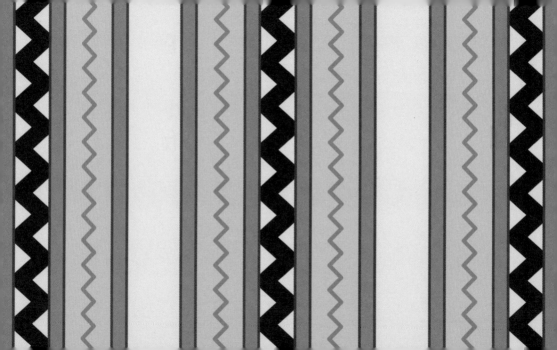

Man Cannot Live By Chocolate Alone— But Woman Sure Can!

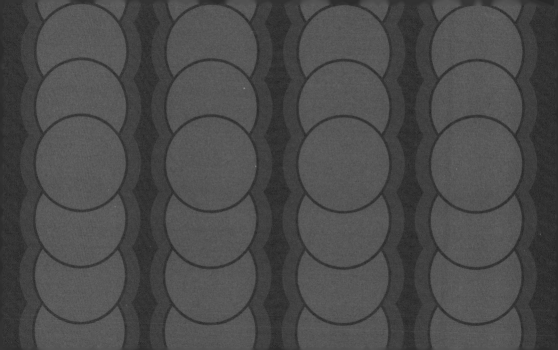

YOU
SAY
TOMATO

I SAY
FUCK YOU

I'll have a
Café-Mocha-
Vodka-Valium-
Latte to go,
please.

ABOUT THE AUTHORS

ED POLISH is the owner of Ephemera, Inc., a novelty company specializing in magnets, buttons, stickers, and other products. Ed has vivid false memories of Satanic rituals at day care, alien probes, and being a spoiled and miserable child star. He is now recuperating in Ashland, Oregon, with his enchanting bride, Ginny. To buy his designs, visit www.ephemera-inc.com.

DARREN WOTZ does his best to appear productive to the untrained eye. Sarcasm is just one of the services he offers. He lives in Berkeley, California, and New York City.